How To

MAKE A
MILLION

By ROWLAND MORGAN

Illustrated by
Judy Brown

FRANKLIN WATTS
A Division of Scholastic Inc.
New York Toronto London Auckland Sydney
Mexico City New Delhi Hong Kong
Danbury, Connecticut

First published 2001 by Oxford University Press
Great Clarendon Street, Oxford OX2 6DP

First American edition 2001 by Franklin Watts
A Division of Scholastic Inc.
90 Sherman Turnpike
Danbury, CT 06816

Catalog details are available from the Library of Congress
Cataloging-in-Publication Data

ISBN 0-531-14638-3 (lib. bdg.) 0-531-14819-X (pbk.)

Printed in China

Contents

A FAST BUCK
How to Make a Billion ....

Six long-haired college friends in California liked to order burritos and play around on their computers together in a garage. They lived in the San Francisco Bay Area. This area is known as Silicon Valley, because computer chips are made out of silicon, and lots of computer companies are based there.

On February 28, 1993, the friends were in Rosita's Taqueria, a Mexican food place near where they lived, discussing how to help people surf the Internet. They decided to invent a software tool that would search millions of Web sites by subject. They went off to their student library at Stanford University to find out how to do it.

Bonehead Bankers ....

In their spare time, while working at other jobs, they wrote some software that grew into a search engine for browsing the Internet. When they had it working, they were so excited that they started calling bankers to ask for money to promote their product to Internet surfers.

Not one of the bankers understood their invention. It was a painful year and a half of wasted time before they found bankers willing to back them.

Astounding Hit ....

At last, the six friends launched their Web site, _http://www.excite.com_, on the Internet in October 1995. In early 1996, advertisers were paying $145,000 to show their name on the Web site. At the end of the year, that income had risen to $14 million—an astounding success story.

The Big Payoff.................................

In 1997, the friends moved to a big office near
Rosita's restaurant to house their two hundred
workers. Millions of Web surfers started visiting
excite.com to find their way around the Web. Because
so many people used it, the site became very valuable.
In 1999, a TV cable company bought Excite Inc. for
$15 billion, and the six founders became super-rich.
Now they have plenty of cash to spend on burritos
and buckets of their favorite drink, Odwalla.

How to Lose a Billion ....

Nick Leeson was a
working-class English
boy who failed math at
school. Somehow he got
a job as a humble clerk
with Coutts, the rich
people's bank, and then
with another small, posh
bank, called Barings.

Slow at school, Nick learned fast at work. At the age of twenty-six, he was in Singapore, betting the bank's money on how the values of Japanese stocks would move (up or down). He was so lucky that in his first year he brought in one-tenth of all the bank's profits. His bosses paid him well.

Disaster Hits.....................................

Japan had a terrible earthquake. Stock-market prices fell. Leeson had gambled on the prices' rising. He lost money but hid the losses in a secret account. He hired a computer expert to stop the computer from warning the bank automatically. He persuaded his unsuspecting bosses to send him more money. He gambled even bigger amounts, to try to drive prices back up.

If you could just give me another £100 million, that would do the trick.

The Boss Finds Out ....

In 1995, Leeson was exposed. He had lost £850 million, or $1.3 billion. Barings bank could not pay. It was ruined. A Dutch bank bought it for about $1.50.

Even Queen Elizabeth II lost money in the collapse. Leeson served four years in a Singapore prison. He got cancer and nearly died, but eventually returned to England. A film of his life, starring Ewan McGregor, was made. Not long ago Leeson earned $88,500 for giving a talk.

In this book, you will find out about

$ what money is

$ the history of money

$ where it's going

$ how it can come your way

$ why the best things in life are free

In this book, you *won't* find out about

$ how to forge banknotes

$ burglary techniques

$ how to hack into online banks

$ maps of hidden treasure

$ how to gamble and win

CHAPTER ONE

WHAT IS A MILLION?

Take a thousand.

A million is a thousand of them. That's a thousand times a thousand times $1.

Plenty, you might say. And if you only have a few coins to your name, it sure is plenty. But these things are relative. Compared to the price of a can of soda (about $.85), $1 million is a huge amount. But compared to the $92 million that rock star David Bowie earned in a recent year, $1 million is relatively little—less than a week's income.

If you got paid $1,000 an hour for going to school, it would take you five months to earn $1 million.

But if you inherited a family house in New York City, you could easily earn $1 million the moment you sold it.

Compare that with the world's most expensive painting, the *Portrait of Dr. Gachet*, by Vincent Van Gogh. It sold for $82.5 million in 1990. Incidentally, that's $82.5 million more than Van Gogh made for his paintings while he was alive.

What You Could Get for $1 Million.........

$ a stack of copies of this book 1 mile (1.5 kilometers) high

$ a line of 83 new family cars

$ a stack of CDs as high as a 100-story skyscraper

$ $30 of pocket money a day for 90 years

Gangsters often wonder whether $1 million would fit into a suitcase. It would take a very big duffle bag. Enough $50 bills to make $1 million would weigh 66 pounds (30 kilograms)—a heavy load, but possible to carry.

The easiest way to store a million, though, is as numerals in a bank account. They would stretch conveniently between these two arrows: ❯   ❮. And they would weigh nothing at all.

CHAPTER TWO

WHAT IS MONEY?

What is the difference between a scrap of newspaper and a piece of paper labeled $50?

Cheap Money

A bill, or banknote, costs pennies to produce. A newspaper costs a few cents more but provides hundreds of times more information. Nevertheless, the next morning the newspaper is good for nothing better than lighting fires. A bill, however, is still worth the amount printed on it. Unlike a piece of newspaper, a banknote will go on being used for between one and four years.

Just like newspapers, banknotes are printed at a factory. The U.S. Bureau of Engraving and Printing produces 22.5 million notes every day. Placed end to end, the notes printed in a year would stretch halfway to the moon.

Trust Me ....

The only difference between an old piece of newspaper and a $50 bill is this. Nobody believes an old piece of newspaper is worth $50. Everybody agrees a $50 bill is.

A shop assistant is willing to part with a cool pair of running shoes or a watch in return for a piece of paper with "$50" written on it. No shop assistant will accept an old piece of newspaper for the goods.

In other words, we *trust* that note to be worth the amount written on it. Bankers have a special word for it. They call the take-it-on-trust banknote "fiduciary." Without trust, you might as well light the fire with your wad of savings.

At one time, a banknote could be exchanged for coins made of gold, silver, and copper. Bills had "I promise to pay the bearer" written on them. More about that later.

Read on for more about banknotes:

$ how they lose value

$ how electronic money replaces them

Pretend Money ....

Money is one of our fundamental inventions, like writing, or the wheel. It's a game of make-believe played by a community. "Let's pretend this whale's tooth is an orange." "Let's pretend this whale's tooth is an apple." If we agree on that, it means an apple and an orange have the same price (1 tooth). If I want to get five apples from you, I no longer need to barter (or exchange) five bulky oranges, available only in a certain season. Instead, I can produce from my handy purse five little whale's teeth.

Will this buy the whole apple orchard?

Someone, somewhere, some time must have been the first person on Earth to hold up a bead and proclaim, "Let's say this is worth one rabbit." But we will never know who that clever character was.

The play-money idea caught on fast. There have been all kinds of agreed-upon currencies used for money. Shells were common in many societies. Teeth were widely used—sometimes dogs' teeth, sometimes whales'. People could wear their bank accounts around their necks. Anything will do for money, although things that are small and don't rot are best. People use other things as money when normal money is not available. People in prison use cigarettes.

Today, the official currency is "legal tender," meaning it is backed by the government. There is nothing to stop anyone from launching their own type of money, however. People just have to agree on its value. Gift certificates from stores are a kind of private money.

Live and Let Live ....

Could we ever follow the example of the ancient Egyptians, who lived pretty happily for about three thousand years without using much money at all? Or could we go back to a system of shells as currency?

Make a Million
PICK UP A MILLION SHELLS

Around 1000 B.C. or earlier

Find a deserted beach. Identify the most common shell on it. Go back to your town and persuade everybody to accept your shell as their currency. Take a bucket and collect a million of them from your beach. Don't tell anyone else where it is.

CHAPTER THREE

MINTING MONEY

Coins and Kings ....

Over time, people started to live in cities, and the power of rulers grew. Different tribes had to accept each other's money. Dealers in silver and gold quickly realized that a standard unit of precious metal could become a widespread currency. Kings and queens liked the idea, and the coin was born.

Silver and gold were already precious metals (because they are soft and do not rust). But deals with silver and gold had to be done by assaying (checking purity by scratching with a "touchstone") and weighing the metals. That was a pain. It was far easier to count units of identical weight.

As Rich as Croesus
Lydia, Turkey, sixth century B.C.

Croesus was king of Lydia (now part of Turkey) 2,500 years ago. He was a very wealthy man, even for a king, because gold and silver could easily be found in the rivers that ran through his kingdom. One day he had a very good idea. He would use some of his gold and silver to make flat discs, all of the same size and weight, and swap them for the goods he wanted to buy. He was pretty sure people would take them, and they did.

King Croesus's coins showed not the king's face, but the national symbol, a lion, facing a raging bull. The symbol assured both the value of the precious metal and the strength of the currency.

A Fine Profile

Ancient queens often looked at their reflections in mirrors of polished silver. Perhaps it was a queen who suggested that a leader replace the usual royal symbol with a person's image. Sculptors trained in Egypt were at that time astonishing the Greek world with their portraits in stone.

Lysimachus, the general who conquered part of modern-day Turkey and Greece, honored Alexander the Great with a portrait on his coins. Ptolemy, leader of Egypt, was the first ruler to create coins with the image of a living person: himself.

Coins were the first mass media, kind of like tiny TVs. Rulers used symbols and pictures to advertise their power. For example, when Rome defeated southern Britain in A.D. 43, a coin was minted to announce the victory to the empire.

The Problem with Cash ....

The word "cash" comes from a French word for chest *(caisse)*. If you had a lot of coins, they were heavy and had to be carried around in a secure box. Rich people slept with their chest under their bed.

Make a Million
SELL PADLOCKS

Europe, the Middle Ages

Design and build good padlocks. Everybody with lots of cash needs a padlock for his or her money chest.

Coins were standard units, and they transformed business as much as computers are doing today. But how standard were they? Say you're a trader. You're handling 100 silver coins. If you shave off 1/100 of each coin, too little to be noticed in routine trading, you still have the face value of 100 coins, plus the precious-metal value of another whole coin.

That is what clipping is. In the early days of coins, clipping was a big problem.

To put a stop to this, the mints that produced the coins began to "mill" their edges with ridges, so that they could tell if the coins had been messed with. This was a good idea, and it has lasted. Check the coins in your wallet: aside from the ones that aren't worth very much, all of them have a scored rim.

Another trick is called sweating. You put your coins in a chest and rattle them around. When you remove them after a good long shaking, metal chips and dust can be scraped off the sides of the chest.

The coins only look a little more worn. The king's profile is still there. The coins still hold their "face" value. You have the gold or silver dust as a bonus.

Funnily enough, while money was more symbolic, like shells or dogs' teeth, there was no advantage in doctoring it. Only when it came in the form of precious metal was it worth tampering with. Today, there is nothing to be gained from clipping a piece off a banknote.

Silver Linings

Silver is a metal that occurs naturally. If you live in the right place, you can find silver dust or even rare nuggets on the ground or in riverbeds. There is still silver lying around rivers in Peru and Norway, for example.

In prehistoric times, people noticed that, like gold, silver does not rust (but it does tarnish, particularly if it comes into contact with eggs). This gave it high practical value for jewelry, cutlery, plates, mirrors, and other objects. Silver also has a magical quality. Wizards associated it with the shiny white moon.

I keep telling you not to get egg on the plates!

About four thousand years ago, someone in China had the idea of making a miniature barter object, such as a spade or a knife, out of bronze. You might not be able to dig with it, but it would never rust away.

About fifteen hundred years later, the people of ancient Greece—who knew nothing about China—had the idea of using silver, a soft and more valuable metal than bronze, to stamp out fixed weights called coins. Many different kinds of coins were made. Trade flourished, and Europe's founding civilization blossomed around the silver *drachma* (handful). Silver literally helped establish urban life.

Silver soon directly changed the course of history, too, because the Greeks developed a big silver mine near Athens. The *drachmas* made from it were spent on building the Greek navy that dramatically reduced the power of Persia.

As power moved to the great city of Rome, so did coinage. Again, silver changed the course of history when Rome had its long struggle with the invasions of Hannibal. Rome launched the silver *denarius* to finance its wars. The strength of this currency helped defeat Carthage, because the money of Carthage couldn't buy as many supplies and armaments.

Silver even played a role in the Christian story. In the Bible, Matthew's Gospel says Judas Iscariot took "thirty pieces of silver" from the chief priest to betray Jesus of Nazareth.

Two Thousand Years of Silver ....

Europe's silver coinage lasted for nine hundred years. Northern Europe used the mark or the franc. In Anglo-Saxon Britain, 240 silver sterlings made a pound-weight of silver. Another silver coin was called the penny. Coins like these lasted until the 1700s.

A big shake-up came when Spain invaded the Americas in the late 1400s and discovered huge deposits of silver. Silver is found naturally in Peru, and Mexico has huge seams of silver-bearing ore. Soon, Spanish galleons were transporting precious cargoes of silver across the Atlantic. Spain issued the *peso duro,* a silver coin that was widely used in the New World.

The dollar was originally named after the German *thaler* (pronounced "tah-ler"). From 1795 to 1965, it was primarily a silver coin. In 1965, the coin's worth as silver became more than one dollar, and it was soon taken out of circulation.

Today few of the world's silver-colored small-change coins actually contain any silver at all. After nearly three thousand years, the "metal of the moon" no longer plays a significant part in the value of money. Mexico, however, continues to produce more silver than any other country.

PURE GOLD

Gold is rare. But if you look in the right place, it can be found easily enough. It glitters in the sand and gravel of many rivers that flow out of mountains.

Make a Million
PAN FOR GOLD

First, prospect a river for gold dust. You can see its tiny flakes of metallic yellow in the gravel of the riverbed. All you need is a bowl. Fill the bowl with gravel or sand from the bottom of the river. Hold it under gently flowing water and swirl it around. The light gravel is gradually washed off, and the gold particles are left near the center of the bowl.

Make a Million
PLACER-MINE GOLD

("Placer" means on the spot.)

First, you must not care about wrecking a beautiful mountain river and threatening or even destroying its precious wildlife, such as migrating salmon that use the gravel for spawning. If you are so greedy for gold that you don't mind, then you hose the gravel away and send it down sluices, which separate the gold dust. Or you could rip up the riverbed and pass it through screens. Many mountain rivers have been degraded by placer gold mining.

Make a Million
DIG FOR GOLD

Gold is often found in underground seams of ore with other metals, such as silver or lead. Gold can be extracted from the ore by dissolving it with mercury or cyanide. Unfortunately, both of these solvents are deadly poisons. A lake of cyanide solution at a big central European gold mine broke its banks in early 2000. It took two days to block the flow of poison, and thousands of animals were killed.

There are even 9 billion tons of gold in the world's seawater. It will probably stay there, however, because extracting it would cost more than it is worth.

Ancient Gold ....

Gold is probably the oldest metal known to humans. It is too soft to make into weapons, but it's easy to make into jewelry and never rusts. From earliest times, it was magically linked to the sun. Artists of ancient Egypt beat gold into paper-thin sheets to adorn their sculptures. The famous gold-covered death mask of Tutankhamen was rediscovered after 3,280 years, still shining. The golden-calf idol described in the Bible's book of Exodus was made at the same time, perhaps by Israelites trained in Egypt.

The Super-Rich
King Midas
Phrygia, 700–400 B.C.

The legend of the "Midas touch" tells of the kings of Phrygia, who turned everything they touched into gold. This story may well refer to the development of placer-mining for gold, and the extraction of gold from plentiful *electrum,* a natural mixture of silver and gold.

➤

Cleopatra
Egypt, 30 B.C.

Queen Cleopatra VII of Egypt still rates as one of the richest women ever. She owned a big share of all the gold ever mined in Africa. She had antiques in her palaces and temples dating back over two thousand years. She controlled the world's only major library, in Alexandria, effectively owning all knowledge. She had also raided the ancient kingdom of Armenia and carried off a huge cargo of treasure. At every meal, she had hundreds of guests, exotic foods, music, and dancing. She spoke several languages and lived with the Roman leader Julius Caesar and, years later, with Caesar's favorite general, Mark Antony. When Caesar's adopted son, the first Roman emperor Augustus, invaded Egypt, Cleopatra's wealth (and the crops of her fertile Egyptian realm) propelled Rome into world domination.

I thought we'd have a nice quiet meal: just the two of us, 50 musicians, 100 dancers, 20 servants...

Caesar's Gold ....

After Augustus conquered Egypt, the Roman emperors (who were all called "Caesar" after Julius Caesar) used the wealth to found their strong golden coinage, the *aureus* (golden), and later the *solidus*.

Emperor Diocletian decreed that all money be measured against gold. His decree was the basis of European money for over a thousand years, and *solidus* was a name in British money until 1971.

Renaissance ....

For a thousand years, Rome was the only country to produce gold coins. Then, in 1235, the first silver florin was struck in Florence, Italy. The bankers there were as independent and innovative as everyone else involved in the budding Renaissance. Up until that year, minting coins had been the exclusive right of the Holy Roman emperor. Now, the progressive citics of northern Italy decided to go it alone. Other cities across Europe followed their cxample, and trade flourished. People exchanged ideas along with goods. They learned to read and write, and began to question the rule of the church in Rome. The modern European states we know today started to emerge. In a way all this change was powered by trade, which itself was based on a trusted gold coinage.

African Gold

Europe's gold mining was still backward in early Renaissance times. Much of the gold for new coins was imported from Africa. Ghana had exported gold for a thousand years. An Arab writer said that gold "grows in the desert like carrots."

The empire of Mali produced "mountains of gold." Most of it was loaded onto caravans of camels. Passing through Timbuktu, the camels carried the gold 1,245 miles (2,000 km) across the Sahara Desert to the ports of Morocco. There, Moors sold it to Europe's bold new bankers.

Spanish Treasure

Greedy for gold, Spaniards invaded the Aztec empire of Mexico in 1519. They found large amounts of it. Later, invading the Inca empire in Peru, they found the Inca king had great roomfuls of solid-gold furniture and ornaments. After this, the search for gold became a kind of fever. The legend of El Dorado, or city of gold, took hold.

The Super-Rich
King Philip II of Spain
Europe and North America, sixteenth century

Philip II, king of Spain, ranks high in the all-time super-rich hall of fame. When his father died, Philip inherited vast estates all over Europe, plus the gold and silver mines of the Americas. His four power-marriages brought him control of Portugal; England; France, most of the Netherlands, Italy, Spain, and the New World; and Austria and much of central Europe.

I take thee, France, Spain, Italy, and America.

Make a Million
PLUNDER A SPANISH GALLEON IN THE SIXTEENTH CENTURY

Find backers in the city of London. Charter a ship, complete with a bloodthirsty but honest crew. Sail the Spanish main (Carribbean Sea), taking care to follow the trade routes. Find a Spanish galleon laden with gold, and plunder it. But make sure your crewmen don't pocket your booty—Queen Elizabeth I lost a lot of money that way to the pirates of Dartmouth.

The Golden State ....

California was a sleepy backwater in 1848, far removed from the revolutions upsetting Europe. It had fewer than twenty thousand inhabitants, all subjects of Mexico. Early that year, a German pioneer named John Sutter decided to build a sawmill. Digging the foundation, workers uncovered lumps of quartz with great chunks of gold in them.

Everyone went crazy. Sutter had hit a seam so rich that in the next five years it yielded twenty-one times more gold than the entire country had ever produced. The seam became known as the Mother Lode.

Word of the Mother Lode spread quickly. By 1849, more than 100,000 prospectors were rushing to California. Farmworkers abandoned their fields, and sailors left their ships. Most prospectors were single men eager to make their fortune and go home. The mining camps were hellish places. Mob lynchings were common, and camps had grim names like Hell's Half-Acre, Rough 'n' Ready, and Hangtown. Criminals ran free. Ten thousand prospectors died of disease or starvation in the first year.

Welcome Stranger ....

Only two years later, Australia struck gold. Here the camps were more widely spread than in California, and there were regulations so strict that they caused an armed revolt by the miners.

A giant nugget weighing 156 pounds (70 kg), as much as a person, was uncovered by a wagon wheel in Australia in 1869. They named it Welcome Stranger.

The Rand ....

The biggest gold mine of all was discovered in 1884.
It was called the Rand. The gold rush that followed
made a boom town of Johannesburg, South Africa,
and triggered the notorious wars in which Britain
attacked the peaceful Boer farmers to seize their gold
field. In the 1930s, the mineshafts reached an amazing
2.5 miles (4 km) deep.

The Klondike ....

In 1896, prospectors rushed to Canada's Yukon
Territory. A rich placer deposit of gold had been
discovered in Bonanza creek on the remote Klondike
River. Outfitters in San Francisco made fortunes
selling equipment, but many prospectors were ruined
by the grueling mountain trek or robbed of their dust.
The tales of storyteller Jack London vividly portray
their adventures.

Gold was the coinage by which all others were measured for nearly two thousand years. However, bankers started to disagree about the gold standard soon after World War I (1914–18). Gold never recovered, and now currencies are valued against each other instead. Today, several metals are more valuable than gold, including platinum and palladium.

Make a Million
WRITE A BEST-SELLER
California, 1849

Write a history of California and sell it to the bored Forty-Niners, as the gold prospectors who rushed to California in 1849 were called. That's what bookseller Hubert Bancroft did. Although California had little history, he wrote dozens of follow-up volumes and made a fortune.

I'm gonna shoot you, then you'll have to put me in your book.

CHAPTER FIVE

PAPER MONEY

During the Middle Ages, goldsmiths used to store gold for merchants. But they noticed that the merchants rarely came to collect their savings. So the goldsmiths started lending the gold out. Then they stopped lending the gold itself, and just wrote IOUs on paper. Soon, instead of paying with gold, merchants started paying with the IOUs. Paper money had been born.

Promises, Promises ....

The banknote in your wallet (if you've got one) is still a kind of IOU. Some countries' currencies actually have a promise written on them. Today that promise is barely worth the paper it's written on, however.

I promise to pay the bearer of this £100 note three pence.

Chief Cashier Central Bank

Until the 1920s, the chief cashier's promise was an IOU for nearly a pound of shiny gold. Now, because a pound of gold is worth tons more than the value of your banknote, it's nothing more than a promise to replace your mangled banknote with a new one.

Fakes

Counterfeiting (or faking) goes way back. As soon as the Bank of England was launched in 1694, Daniel Perrismore got busy faking its handwritten banknotes. He transcribed at least sixty notes of £100. Each was worth five times a typical annual income at the time. Today that would be about £100,000. People had long been hanged for faking coins, but for some reason Perrismore got off lightly. He was only fined and pilloried. Shortly afterward, hanging became the sentence for passing a counterfeit note—even if a person thought the note was genuine. Even when hanging was abolished for passing counterfeit notes in the 1830s, you could still get a life sentence in prison.

I'm Daniel Perrismore—I've come to pay my fine.

Banknote Bombs ·······························

Counterfeit money is a weapon of war. People have printed loads of phone notes and dropped them from planes over enemy territory. The idea is to wreck the value of the enemy's currency. That makes it harder for them to buy supplies with which to fight you. People love having money dropping out of the sky. In World War II (1939–45), Nazi Germany printed half a million "British" banknotes every month.

Make a Million
GET A PATENT ON BANKNOTES
World War II

Dream up a process for embedding a metal thread in paper money. National banks will introduce it as a security measure. Your patent on the process will make you a wartime star.

Anti-Fake Gadgets ·····················

Can't you just put a $20 bill on a color copier?

Sorry, it's not as easy as that. Today's banknote may only cost three pennies to make, but it is loaded with anti-faking devices—read on.

Special paper. Made of cotton. Crisp and slightly rough in the printed areas. Not limp, waxy, or shiny.

Threads. Small blue and red fibers are embedded in the paper.

Federal Reserve indicators.

Denomination. This number indicates what the bill is worth.

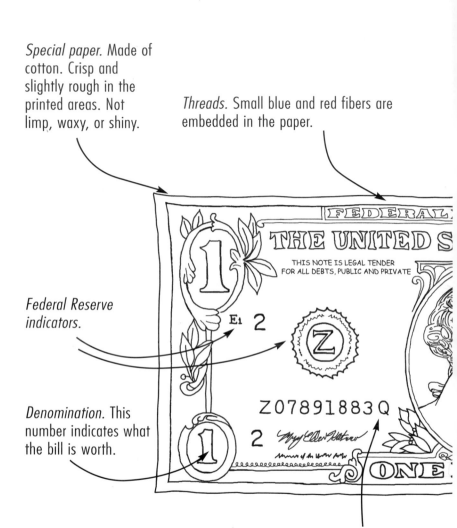

Serial number. Composed of numbers and letters, it identifies each individual note.

Portrait. U.S. bills have portraits of major historical figures. The $1 bill features George Washington.

Super-quality printing. Fine lines that are sharp and well-defined, with pure and clear colors.

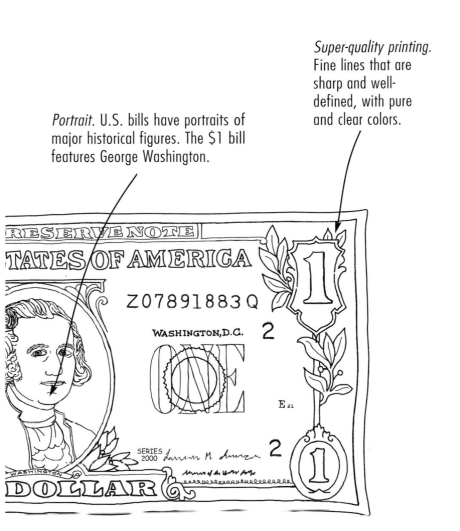

Secret features. Sorry, we can't write about them. Your mission (should you choose to accept it) is to find out what they are. If you're successful, please give us a call before the FBI calls you.

Banknote FAQs* ....

The largest banknote ever printed was the Gold Certificate of 1934, worth $100,000. The bill featured a portrait of President Woodrow Wilson. None of these bills was ever seen outside of the Federal Reserve banks.

The Secretary of the Treasury decides on the designs. An interesting fact: it is against the law for living people to be printed on U.S. banknotes.

Not for public circulation, no. However, some people have been puzzled to come into possession of a "One Million Dollar Special Issue" note. These were actually

---

"platinum certificates" sold by a Canadian for one dollar each as a collectible item. He was reported to the FBI, which decided he had not violated any United States law. No hanging for him!

What should I do if I notice I have been given a counterfeit banknote?

Sternly talk to the person who passed it to you. He or she has committed a criminal offense. If they won't take it back, or you don't know who they are, call the police station. Promise the police you did NOT make it yourself.

How can I get hold of banknotes?

Ask people for them. Or drop hints. At Christmas, write "banknotes." They're notes you mail to people saying, "It's Christmas. Go to the bank."

How to Print Your Own Banknotes ....

1. Get hold of a printing factory and surround it with security officers and dangerous dogs.

2. Spend years planning, designing, and drawing one banknote. It should show a portrait of someone who has made a huge contribution to your nation and to the world, like Martin Luther King, Jr., or a member of 'NSync.

3. Obtain watermarked paper with embedded thread that flashes under ultraviolet light. Take note: the person selling it to you will have dark glasses, a black hat, and overcoat, and bouncers standing on each side of him.

4. Attach eight plates onto your lithographic printing press and run off 1.3 billion notes, leaving out the portrait, the lettering, and the numbering. Do not try to buy anything with these yet. People might notice the gaps.

5. Now use a special intaglio press to suck the portrait and the lettering onto the front of your notes under a pressure of 15 tons per square inch.

6. Before adding serial numbers, check through the 1.3 billion notes for flaws. That means looking through a stack of notes 170 miles (433 km) high, by the way. (That's how many banknotes mints make a year, so why shouldn't you?) Incidentally, this is all done by staff examining each note.

7. Now go to your letterpress. This resembles the machine invented by Herr Gutenberg in 1439 and stolen from him by his partner, Herr Fust. Use it to print serial numbers on the notes. Print a different one on every note, remember. Still feeling confident about this?

8. Now use your production-line equipment to guillotine the notes apart, shrink-wrap them into packages of hundreds and then thousands. At this point, you might wish to stuff a few of the bundles into your pockets.

9. Send the parcels out to your bank branches. Distribute the notes according to public demand. You'll need a line of huge trucks 5.5 miles (9 km) long to transport all the bills.

CHAPTER SIX

GREAT CURRENCIES

THE DOLLAR

Colonial Americans used coins from many different countries. Colonists also used bullets, tobacco, and animal skins as money. U.S. revolutionaries adopted the dollar's name from the widely trusted Spanish "hard dollar," used all over North and South America.

The dollar got off to a bad start. The first notes were printed to finance the American Revolution in 1776. People soon realized there were more notes than gold coins to back them, and the notes became worthless.

Silver and gold coins gave the fledgling currency many problems. For example, if the gold coins were valued too low, gold was worth more as bullion (raw metal). Or silver dollars could be exported to the West Indies and swapped directly for Spanish dollars, which were heavier. They could then be melted down, taken back to the United States, and made back into U.S. dollars at a profit. Eventually gold became the standard.

The U.S. gold reserves are stored at Fort Knox in Kentucky. The fort is an enormous military zone (32,120 acres, or 300 times the size of New York City's Central Park), bristling with hundreds of armored vehicles and thousands of soldiers. In the middle of it is the U.S. Gold Depository, a fortified building with a vault beneath it.

In this vault is stored much of the U.S. government's huge golden treasure. Thousands of gold ingots stand in stacks, guarded by heavily armed officers. The reserve is said to be worth well over $6 billion.

Who Is Susan B. Anthony? ....

Susan B. Anthony was a suffragette who fought for women's right to vote. She campaigned for fifty years and died in 1906. Fourteen years later, women were granted the vote by the Nineteenth Amendment. The first woman to appear on a US coin, Anthony was on the silver dollar from 1979 to 1981. No woman has yet appeared on American paper currency.

Pictures on Dollar Bills ....

$1   George Washington
(first U.S. president)
and Great Seal of
the United States

$2   Thomas Jefferson
(author of the
Declaration of
Independence,
third U.S. president)

$5   Abraham Lincoln (U.S. president during the
Civil War) and Lincoln Memorial

$10   Andrew Hamilton (first secretary of the
treasury) and U.S. Treasury building

$20   Andrew Jackson (seventh U.S. president) and
the White House

$50   Ulysses S. Grant (Civil War general) and the
Capitol building

$100   Benjamin Franklin (diplomat and inventor) and
Independence Hall

THE POUND ....

The Industrial Revolution started in Britain. Products marked "Made in England" (even if they were made in Wales, Scotland, or Ireland) were sold worldwide. Naturally, the currency that backed them became the most trusted, which is the same as being the strongest. The pound was such a strong currency that it remained at the same high value for nearly a hundred years, from the end of the war with France in 1815 to the beginning of World War I in 1914.

The £5 Note ....

The £5 note was printed on a large piece of crisp white paper. Its inscription was in fancy copperplate face. There were no pictures or decorations. It was like a personal letter of recommendation from the chief clerk of the Bank of England.

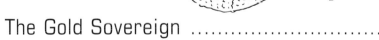

The Gold Sovereign ....

This was a coin to treasure. Made of 90 percent pure gold (if it had been all gold it would have been too soft), it was possibly the most valuable coin ever minted for general circulation. One sovereign, a little bigger than today's penny, was a decent English income for a week. Overseas it was worth many times more. First made in 1489, it was finally withdrawn in 1914. Its gold was generally imported from Guinea in Africa, so "guinea" was the name of its companion gold piece (1663–1813). In 1845, a guinea bought more than a ton of coal in London.

The Victorian Penny ···························

This once-famous coin was bigger than today's 50-cent piece. Beautifully made of copper, for many years it had a flattering profile of a girlish Queen Victoria on one side (her prominent nose was doctored). It bought a first-class postage stamp or a pound of potatoes.

Make a Million
START A FOOD FAD
1890s

Start a fad for a health food. Vegetarian fanatic Dr. Harvey Kellogg and his brother Will, based in Florida, invented corn flakes in the 1890s and made a fortune.

Make a Million
FIND A PLACE IN THE SUN
Early twentieth century

Go to Nice in the south of France. With your pounds sterling, everything costs next to nothing in this sleepy fishing village. Buy a few beaches and live in luxury. Wait until aristocrats flock after you in search of the warm, sunny winter. Sell them waterfront building plots for hundreds of times what you paid. Many of the British did just that.

THE YEN ....

Japan cut ties with the outside world in the 1600s to keep Christian missionaries out. It did not start trading with foreigners until 1854, long after the Industrial Revolution had started. Then the Japanese decided to catch up. They launched the yen currency in 1871 (from Chinese *yuen*, meaning "round"). They based their silver coin on the Mexican peso and their gold coin on the U.S. dollar.

Japan defeated Russia in war and became a major industrial power in the early twentieth century. Her economy was ruined in World War II. Then people like Soichiro Honda started new backyard enterprises that became international companies. Backed by names like Sony, Mitsubishi, and Toyota, the yen was a major currency by 2000.

THE MARK ....

Germany's currency is named after an ancient weight of gold (two-thirds of a Roman pound). Marks were the basic coinage of German-speaking peoples, who lived in many small states across northern and central Europe. When Germans founded an empire to compete with Britain's in 1871, its currency was gold coins of 5, 10, and 20 marks. Later, like other countries, Germany launched paper money. However, after World War I, confidence in Germany's paper money collapsed, and the mark suffered the worst inflation ever known. Here's what happened to the price of 1 lb (.5 kg) of butter in 1923:

Price of 18 oz (500g) butter, 1923	January	October 23	November 5
	3,400 marks	26 million marks	280 million marks

That means everyone must have been a millionaire!

The money became almost worthless. For example, postage stamps were printed as 50 million marks. A short bus trip cost 150 million marks. They printed a note of 100 billion marks. In 1924, Germany relaunched the mark as the reichsmark, based partly on gold and partly on Germany's real-estate value (its country, farms, and buildings). After World War II, all debts were wiped out by 90 percent, and the mark was relaunched again, this time as the Deutsche Mark (DM). The economic miracle that followed transformed Germany's troubled currency into Europe's most trusted one. In 2002 it will be replaced by the Euro.

THE EURO ....

The European Union has launched its own currency to replace those of nearly all member countries. Until the start of 2002, it is only marked as a second price on products. In 2002 it will have its own notes and coins. All member countries' currencies already look a lot like the Euro, so the only big change will be the name, the currency symbol (which looks like this: €), and the denominations. The UK, Denmark, Sweden, and Greece are still deciding whether to replace their currencies with the Euro.

Currencies Outside the Euro

Czech Republic: koruna
Denmark: krone
Greece: drachma
Hungary: forint
Russia: ruble
Sweden: Swedish krona
UK: pound

Currencies Joining the Euro

Austria: schilling
Belgium: Belgian franc
Finland: markka
France: franc
Germany: Deutsche Mark
Ireland: Irish pound
Italy: lira
Luxembourg: franc
Netherlands: guilder
Portugal: escudo
Spain: peseta

Nicknames for Currency ....

The $1 bill
$ Buck
$ Greenback
$ Smacker
$ Frogskin

The $5 bill
$ Finn
$ Five-case note
$ Half-saw
$ V-spot

The $10 bill
$ Dew
$ Double finn
$ Sawbuck
$ Short bit

The $100 bill
$ C-note

The $1000 bill
$ G-note
$ Grand
$ Horse
$ Ten yards

Currencies with Interesting Names ....

Baht (Thailand)	Balboa (Panama)
Carbovanets (Ukraine)	Dong (Vietnam)
Kwacha (Zambia)	Metical (Mozambique)
Zloty (Poland)	Kyat (Myanmar)

CHAPTER SEVEN

INVESTING YOUR MONEY

Now that gold is no longer the standard of money's value, all currency is backed by investments. The value of a currency note is fixed; it does not grow. For your money to grow in value, you need to invest it: you need "near money." Near money consists of bonds, stocks, insurance, and mortgages.

Is that what they mean by near money?

Bonds and Stocks ....

A bond is an IOU. Governments and companies offer them for sale in order to raise money. If you buy a bond (from a bank or through the stock market), you get an interest payment every year. This is like collecting rent on the money that you lent by buying the bond. An 8 percent bond with a face value of $1000 will pay $80 a year. There are many different types of bond, but as they all have fixed interest and face value, you're not going to make a million this way.

If you want to make a million, consider buying stocks. A stock is a certificate that proves you own a piece of a company (like Ford, Sony, or Mattel). In other words, it is a share in the company. Your share has a value that goes up and down with the success of the company.

You could make a fortune. You could also lose it all. A common way to play it safe is to let stockbrokers buy shares for you. They choose the companies they think will do well. Even this is risky, of course.

Investing in the stock market is a bit like gambling. Shares go up and down in value. You are taking a risk with your money. However, most shareholders don't lose. A long-term investment in stock, between ten and twenty years, has shown a good increase since World War II. Short-term investments, from a few days to a year or two, are more risky.

Make a Million
INVEST IN SHELL
(NOT SHELLS)
1925

Invest $50 in Shell Oil Company shares today, and live until 1995. You could sell the shares for thousands of times what you paid for them.

Insurance

An insurance policy is a contract in which an insurer promises to pay certain costs as long as you make regular payments.

Explain?
You buy a car for $15,000. You pay $750 to insure it. You crash it into another car worth $15,000, destroying both cars. The driver of the other car needs an operation that costs $20,000. You need an operation that costs $10,000. The crash does $50,000 worth of damage to a building. What is your total bill for the crash?

Answer 1: $110,000
Answer 2: $750

The correct answer is Answer 2. Because you paid
$750 for a policy, the insurance company pays out the
$110,000. You save $109,250—a pile of money.

So that's the end of the insurance company, right?

Wrong. Insurance companies make hefty profits.

Here's how they do it. They figure out the average
cost of accidents among, say, a million drivers. Then
they charge you one-millionth of that, plus a bonus for
their profits. They don't know who will have the
crashes, or how much each crash will cost. But they've
got the overall cost covered by the million policies
they've sold. They pay out in each case and still win.

Meanwhile, the insurance company is free to use your
payments to buy stocks. It can make bundles of
money on the side this way.

Mortgages ....

A mortgage is a home loan. The word means "death pledge"—a debt that is probably going to last all your life.

This grim name arises from the gravity of promising to make payments for many years on the roof over your head. If you fail to make the payments, you could end up on the street. A landlord may grant property in exchange for a mortgage, but usually a bank finances the deal. If the house owner then fails to pay, the bank gets the property. When the economic cycle turns down, and many people fail to make mortgage payments, banks seize many homes. This is something bankers prefer not to talk about.

Great Crashes ....

A market economy goes in cycles: bull markets (boom), and bear markets (bust). Mathematicians and computer whizzes try to forecast when they will happen. If they succeed, they keep the secret in order to profit. A big bust, however, is never kept secret, because it is usually preceded by a thrilling boom. By definition, nobody can make money without others losing it. Some crashes have become legendary.

Tulipomania
Holland, 1600s

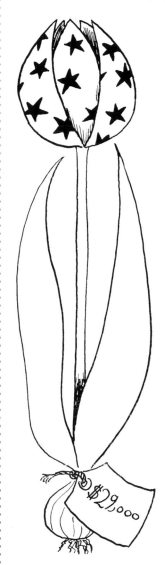

Everybody knows what a tulip looks like, right? They might now, but they didn't in the 1500s, because tulips had never been planted outside of Turkey. Tulips were called *tulipan,* or "turban," in Turkish, a reference to their shape. A Dutch trader had the idea of bringing some tulip bulbs home in the late 1500s. He grew them in the garden, and the neighbors got interested. One thing led to another, and companies started offering shares of stock in things like upside-down tulips, inside-out tulips, and the notorious "black" tulip.

Speculators bought stock, which skyrocketed as bulbs sold for 5,500 gold florins each (about $29,000 today). Eventually it all led to tears. Wealthy people lost all their money because the stock turned out to be worthless (no one ever managed to produce a black tulip, for example). The government had to take over. Tulips are big business in Holland today, but the great tulip fiasco will never be forgotten.

The South Sea Bubble
Britain, 1720

The stock market was born in the early 1700s with a huge scandal that ruined many people. It all started with one of the world's first companies. The British king or queen was in the habit of giving out big chunks of the world to new companies to develop. These new companies had to make as much money as they could for their stockholders. The Hudson's Bay company had a monopoly on trade in Canada, the East India company had Asia, and the Royal African company controlled the thriving—but tragic—trade in African slaves.

The South Sea company controlled trade in South America and the Pacific Islands. The stock was attractive, and many people invested, including the new King George I himself. In 1720, the stock price rocketed from £10 to £100. Greedy investors were falling over each other to buy. However, news went around that the bosses of the company had sold their stock for massive profits. Immediately, people were falling over each other to sell. The South Sea company's stock value collapsed. Shareholders who had paid as much as £100 for stock that was now almost worthless were ruined.

The Wall Street Crash, Part 1

New York City, October 1929

Wall Street is an avenue of towers in New York City. The U.S. stock exchange and many banks have their head offices there. In August 1929, Wall Street was an exciting place. Every day, traders on the floor of the stock exchange went half-crazy shouting at each other because there was so much demand for stock.

Companies were making profits and paying out great dividends (profits) to shareholders, and stock prices were rising rapidly. A few careful investors noticed that dividends were dropping a little as business slowed down. They sold their stock and bought other things, such as buildings or gold. People who weren't in the know greedily rushed to buy stock "in the margin." That meant they paid only 3 percent of the price of the stock and borrowed the rest of the cost from their stockbroker.

Prices went on soaring, attracting yet more ignorant buyers who sold their homes or took out bank loans to buy shares. Many shareholders decided the boom couldn't last and started to sell stock, taking their profit and driving prices down. New shareholders, who had bought at high prices, often with borrowed money, watched in horror as prices started to slide below what they had paid. In a panic, they hurried to sell before the prices dropped any further. That only made prices drop even faster. On October 29, prices collapsed. Thousands of people were completely ruined. Desperate men threw themselves out of skyscraper windows. Ruined bosses shut down their factories. Millions were thrown out of work around the world.

The Wall Street Crash, Part 2

Black Monday, October 19, 1987

Almost fifty-eight years later to the day, U.S. stock prices took a downward plunge that experts had thought impossible. Prices had faltered in the previous week, but few suspected the shock that came after the weekend. Certain items of bad news released that Monday, combined with the slowdown of industry, triggered automatic commands from programs installed in some major investors' computers. Faulty programming meant that the impossible happened, and computers "panicked" just like humans.

➤

The result was that stock prices lost one-fifth of their value in one day. This time, however, those who kept their nerve were rewarded. Stock prices had recovered completely by the end of the year.

Make a Million
MANUFACTURE ARMS
1929–1945

A very dubious way to make money from World War II would have been to buy lots of industrial stock in the United States in 1929 for almost nothing. When the United States got into World War II in 1941, the government spent $341 billion on industry to equip the armed forces. Stock bought cheaply in 1929 was worth billions by 1945.

Banks

Banks got their name from the benches that goldsmiths used to sit on in their shops. Goldsmiths would lend space in their safes for keeping people's gold (this was called "taking a deposit"). They would then lend the gold out to other people (this was called "making a loan"). And that's basically what banks still do today. The main way that banks make their profits is to charge rent (interest) on the money they lend.

Money that banks lend is called credit. Credit means trust. In money, if I extend you credit, I lend you money because I trust you to pay it back. Of course, if I am a bank, I'll require something valuable to stand in for the money I am lending. This is called collateral. So, if a bank lends you a pile of cash to launch a Web site, it will "take a lien" on your house, or whatever else you can offer as security. Then, if you fail to repay the loan as you promised in a contract, the bank can seize your house, sell it, and pay itself back with the money from the sale.

A pawnbroker, who lends money in exchange for second-hand goods, does not have to seize your property if you don't repay. It's already in his shop.

Ninety percent of all American business is done on bank credit. It's known as OPM—other people's money.

By contrast, all the cathedrals of Europe were built without credit. The astonishing pyramids of ancient Egypt, more than sixty of them, were built without credit. Agriculture, writing, the wheel, paper—all were invented and developed without credit.

We discovered earlier that money is just an agreed-upon measure, like feet or yards. Wouldn't it be silly if people sat behind desks and offered to lend people yards? "Wanna build a house? We'll lend you 100,000 square yards!" Well, you could say lending money is equally silly. As if we could ever "run out" of yards!

I can't go any farther—I'm all out of yards, honest!

How Do Banks Make Money? ....

Very simple. They pay less for the money you lend them than you pay for the money they lend you. Explain? If you deposit $40 in your savings account at 10 percent annual interest rate for three years, the bank will pay you $13.24 for it. However, if they deposit $40 in your account, and the interest rate is 17 percent over three years, you pay them $24.06 for the same amount.
Their profit?

$24.06
−$13.24
= $10.82

So there's one rate paid for money coming in, and a much higher rate charged for money going out. Sound like a scam? Many think so. One solution people in England came up with was the building society.

Building Societies ....

Everybody who puts money into a building society becomes a member and receives a share of the earnings. It's a bank owned by its account holders. The building society does not have outside shareholders demanding high dividends, as a bank does. That means they charge lower rent on money they lend. It's an important consideration in the enormous expense of building or buying a house, which is almost everybody's biggest investment.

Internet Banking ....

Both banks and building societies offer Internet
banking. This means you can look after your finances
without ever going into a bank branch.

What the Internet Bank Does ....

An Internet bank is:

CHEAPER. Because the bank has no buildings to maintain, the cost of credit is several percentage points lower, and interest paid on savings is higher. However, there are costs for going online.

LESS FRIENDLY. You will never see anybody who works at the Internet bank, let alone get to know them.

Did you see that game last night? Great, wasn't it?

PRIVATE. If your finances are in a mess, you can blush at the computer—nobody else will see.

CONTROLLED BY YOU. You can do everything your own way—within their software.

LIGHT ON STAFF. An Internet bank employs only about fifteen hundred people.

VULNERABLE TO CRASHES. Then you're stuck.

OPEN 24 HOURS A DAY.

A bank is:

COSTLIER. Because the bank branch has to be built and maintained, interest rates are higher. But going into the branch costs nothing.

FRIENDLIER. "Warm bodies" work at the bank. They might get to know you and even become friends.

PUBLIC. Sometimes banking in public can be embarrassing. You might actually get approached by the manager.

CONTROLLED BY THEM. They do it their way once you've walked in the door.

HEAVY ON STAFF. A bank chain employs about 25,000 people.

NOT GOING TO CRASH. Even if their computer is "down," they'll still do the job.

OPEN 40–50 HOURS A WEEK.

Ninety percent of modern business is done on credit from banks, and people are often in personal debt as well. They use multiple credit cards, which keep a record of their debt. This might seem normal, but it is a risky situation. Credit only lasts as long as payments can be made. If payments stop, so does the credit. Then it can get nasty.

The lender can send in law officers to take away all your furniture and belongings to sell them. If this doesn't cover the debt, you're called bankrupt, which gives you a bad name. You could even go to prison.

The safest course is to save up, plan your expenses, and pay for what you want with your own money.

Personal Finance ....

At one time, people hung their dog's teeth around their necks for everyone to see. Now they keep track of their money in a bank account. You need money coming in (income) so that you can pay your bills (expenditures). Whatever is left (after paying taxes), you can save—or spend!

Hmm... I've saved enough dog's teeth for a necklace.

Savings

Savings can grow surprisingly. Here's a chart of how much certain weekly amounts increase after four years—not counting the interest paid by your savings account.

Weekly amount	After 3 months	After 6 months	After 1 year	After 2 years	After 4 years	After 5 years
$2	24	48	104	208	312	416
$4	48	96	208	416	624	832
$8	96	208	416	832	1,248	1,664

Spend, Spend, Spend!

Credit (which really means debt) drives a consumer economy. The average American is $7,000 in debt to credit companies. According to the Federal Reserve Board, Americans owed more than $450 billion in credit. An American pays on average more in credit card fees in a year than one of the world's poorest people receives in total annual income.

Why do consumers need so much money, and what do they spend it on? Here is a chart of the consumer classes of the world:

World Consumer Classes

	Top consumers (1.1 billion people)	Middle consumers (3.3 billion people)	Poor (1.1 billion people)
What they eat	supermarket meat, packaged foods, soft drinks	grain, clean water	too little grain, not enough water
How they move	private cars, usually carrying one person	bicycles, buses	walking, animals
Their stuff	"disposables"	goods that last	things made from local materials, like wood
Their music	studio-made CDs	folk songs	communal music

Chart: adapted from Worldwatch Institute

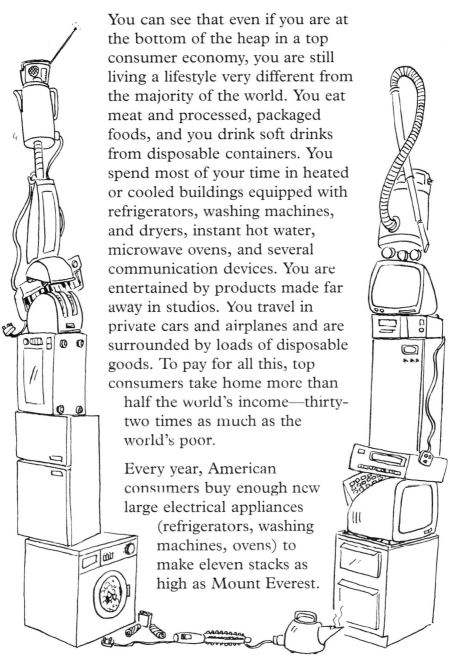

You can see that even if you are at the bottom of the heap in a top consumer economy, you are still living a lifestyle very different from the majority of the world. You eat meat and processed, packaged foods, and you drink soft drinks from disposable containers. You spend most of your time in heated or cooled buildings equipped with refrigerators, washing machines, and dryers, instant hot water, microwave ovens, and several communication devices. You are entertained by products made far away in studios. You travel in private cars and airplanes and are surrounded by loads of disposable goods. To pay for all this, top consumers take home more than half the world's income—thirty-two times as much as the world's poor.

Every year, American consumers buy enough new large electrical appliances (refrigerators, washing machines, ovens) to make eleven stacks as high as Mount Everest.

What We Consume Today ....

These days, many people expect to have a telephone (although most people in the world do not actually have one). Too many of us have cars (they would stack up to the moon!).

Here's what Americans spent on some consumer goods in 1997:

Consumer product	U.S. consumer spending in 1997
Food	$781 billion
Clothing/accessories	$353 billion
Telephones	$104 billion
New/used cars	$143 billion
Movie tickets	$6.6 billion
Spectator sports	$6.7 billion
Books and maps	$25 billion
Magazines, news-papers, sheet music	$29 billion
Higher education	$69.6 billion

Source: Bureau of Economic Analysis, U.S. Department of Commerce

Make a Million
BY CLOCKWORK
1990s

British inventor Trevor Baylis made a million by dreaming up the clockwork radio and the clockwork flashlight. Can you think of any other consumer appliances that could be powered by clockwork? You might make a million. You might also save the environment. Clockwork machines aren't powered by electricity, so they don't add to global warming.

CHAPTER EIGHT

MONEY: HOW TO GET IT

How to Steal a Million ....

Bonehead

Dave Dozey has lots of muscle, but nothing much upstairs. He loves money and has no idea how to make it, apart from stealing it from other people. His plan is to go out and rob a security van. Here are the crimes he has to commit to pull off the job, along with the possible prison sentences:

1. Steal a car for the raid (six months)
2. Steal a getaway car (six months)
3. Possess an illegal firearm (three years)
4. Drive recklessly (three months)
5. Inflict grievous bodily harm (three years)
6. Commit armed robbery (six years)
7. Leave the scene of an accident (three months)
8. Dispose of stolen goods (nine months)

Because Dave is a bonehead, he is embarking on a crime that could cost him over fourteen years of prison time. He is also taking on some 175,000 policemen and another 150,000 security officers who can't wait to catch him. Not only that, he is also taking the following risks:

1. Being assaulted by the owners of the cars
2. Getting hurt in a crash when he blocks the armored van
3. Getting assaulted by a security guard
4. Getting sprayed with mace

5. Shooting himself in the foot during the arrest
6. ·Wrenching a muscle carrying the loot
7. Getting run over hurrying to the getaway car
8. Getting hurt in a crash evading police

Dave is pretty nervous about the job. He sweats a lot, and snaps at his girlfriend. He's not sure what he will do with all the loot. And he's pretty sure he'll be on the run for a long time before he gets any peace of mind.

Brains

Sid Smooth is a wicked thief, but he is not dumb. He has never even considered doing anything so idiotic as trying to pull off a stickup in a public place, then trying to get away with a load of loot in the middle of heavy traffic.

Sid works at a computer. He has mastered several of the most important software languages and taken evening classes in Internet technology. He has spent many enjoyable hours in the comfort of his own home, practicing hacking into the Web sites of banks. He doesn't bother with the big banks—they've built software "firewalls" to keep hackers out. But there are thousands of other banks that haven't caught up, and won't for a long time. When he feels like taking a break, he wanders into his kitchen and brews up some coffee. He might watch a bit of TV before he goes back to work.

Sid is working in a small town in the English Midlands. Using alias identities on the Internet, he has arranged it so that anyone trying to trace him will think he is based in Australia. Unfortunately, there are only a few hundred policemen on the planet who understand what he is doing.

He has opened an Internet bank account under a false name and address in Finland, and several other accounts in obscure places like Liechtenstein and Belize. He did all this without moving from his desk.

Sid has written fiendishly complicated software that quietly removes very small amounts from thousands of online bank accounts around the world and transfers them to his accounts. The program never works very long in one place, and never puts too much money into one of his accounts. Working this way, over the last nine months, Sid has stolen well over $1 million.

Sid has committed many more crimes than Dave Dozey. But he's less likely to get caught. The police and the banks are only just beginning to get a grip on Internet crimes, and it will

probably be a while before they catch up with Sid. He hopes to retire to a comfortable villa in a far-off sunny country before then.

How to Launder Money ....

The big problem with being a criminal is that the money you have made out of crime is dirty (illegal). For example, if you sell a bag of stolen diamonds, you suddenly have a pile of money. You can't explain to a detective where you got it if one comes nosing round. Big-time criminals have suitcases full of dirty money, carloads of it, garages full. They have to get rid of it.

So do they go and spend it on classical paintings and mink coats for dogs? No way! That's the best way to stick out. That kind of stuff is just as suspicious as a pile of money.

What intelligent criminals do with dirty money is clean it up. They launder it.

How? Well, have you got a few weeks? There are so many ways. Here are a couple:

Tow a caravan full of dirty cash to the Yukon Territory in Canada. Go to mines deep in the hills and buy several loads of gold, using a false identity. Drive to various gold bullion dealers, selling a little of your gold at a time so as not to attract attention. Tell them each time it's an heirloom from your old auntie. Get each dealer to write a check to a new business called Whatever Enterprises. Open accounts in different banks in different cities under the Whatever Enterprises name.

Deposit the checks. Buy shops in different places and start selling cellular phones. Place the profits from the shops in a bank account under your own name. Your loot has now been laundered.

Bribe somebody at a film company to let you have a video of a hot new movie. Make thousands of illegal copies of it. Label them as educational films about growing rice. Ship them to China. Re-label and distribute them to street markets. Collect the cash in small amounts weekly and deposit it in a business account in Hong Kong. Transfer the money to various accounts in your name across Europe. Take a long vacation, picking up laundered cash at all your banks.

The best way of all is to transfer your money OFFSHORE...

Crime: Offshore Money ....

Every country has a tax system. Federal and state governments raise taxes mainly for defense, but also for education. Education is necessary because citizens need to be able to read so that they can understand tax forms. (Actually, nobody understands tax forms.) Anyway, people have to pay taxes. Or do they?

Ever since taxes began, people have been evading or avoiding them. Evading is illegal; avoiding is legal. The difference between these two words could be a prison sentence.

The best way to avoid having your money taxed by the state is to keep it outside the state. However, the state you move it to is likely to want to tax it instead. So you have to move it to a funny little place called a "tax shelter," which has very low taxes or none at all. Rich people often don't pay taxes; they put their money in a shelter. So do lots of gangsters. Here are the names of a few shelters. You can look them up in the atlas.

Andorra

Liechtenstein

Cayman Islands

Belize

Make a Million
CREATE YOUR OWN
TAX HAVEN
Today

Find some strange, out-of-the-way place, like a tiny island in the Pacific Ocean. Rent a room there. Connect a computer to the Internet. Call it a bank. Take deposits. Ask no questions. Give no interviews. Sunbathe.

The Super-Rich
Andrew Carnegie: Worked for It

Born into a poor family in Scotland in 1835, Andrew Carnegie immigrated to the United States with his parents. He spent many years as a worker on the railroads. During and after the Civil War, he worked in steel plants. Soon he had his own factory. Then he bought others. By the 1890s, the massive expansion of the United States had made this simple man hugely rich. He retired in 1901 to spend his fortune on libraries, education, and peace. Today Carnegie is remembered as a philanthropist (someone who gives money away).

The Queen of Britain: Inherited It

Queen Elizabeth II was on a state visit to Africa with her husband in 1953 when she learned that her father, the king, had died suddenly. She had inherited five enormous palaces, vast lands, and a huge personal fortune. She was also the constitutional head of Great Britain and the Commonwealth, giving her great power and influence. More huge properties called the Crown estate are administered by the government, so the Queen only half-owns them.

➤

The Queen is among the richest people on Earth, and she manages her wealth well. In the late 1990s, she made a million on the Internet.

Bill Gates: Did a Deal for It

Bill Gates was born in Washington state to well-off parents in 1956. As a teenager, he was interested in business and computers. In his early twenties, he got the chance to buy a little personal computer company. He offered its operating system (the software that allows it to do basic jobs, like sending images to the screen) to the huge business empire IBM. They wanted it for their new line of personal computers. Renting out the Microsoft disk operating system (MS-DOS) made Gates his first fortune, as personal computers spread like

I made it by MS-DOSsing about!

TVs. Later, he and his partner added Windows, Word, NT, Internet Explorer, and Encarta to their range of Microsoft software. Today, 90 percent of the world's computers use these products. Gates became the richest man in the world, with a fortune estimated at about $60 billion.

SUCCESS!

STRICTLY CONFIDENTIAL ✳✳✳ DO NOT BROWSE HERE
✳✳✳ TOP SECRET INFORMATION ✳✳✳

How to Make a Million, Part 1 . . . .

1. Make some adorable, cuddly, furry little puppy-dog toys.

2. Take a photo of your puppy toys looking completely huggable.

3. Create a Web site called _http://www.huggablepuppies.com_.

4. Scan the cuddly toys' photographs onto the Web site. Write all about the toys: their names, their favorite food, and so on. Announce that they are for sale by auction.

5. Tell everybody you know about your Web site.

6. Don't take the first auction bid that comes in. Say "We'll get back to you," and wait for a better offer.

7. Announce on your Web site how much each toy went for. This gives people the idea they can actually get these cuddly toys.

8. Put more pictures of cuddly doggies on your Web site. Expand into other sizes, all cuddly, all adorable.

9. As thousands of people start e-mailing wanting your cuddly toys, ask one of your local Internet cafés to put you in touch with Z-shops®.

10. Open a Z-shop auction room, letting Web-surfers bid for your cuddly toys online.
11. Invite people to submit pictures and stories about their cuddly toys for sale. Publish only pictures of adorable little cuddly puppy toys.
12. When the first offer comes in to buy your Web site, refuse.
13. Tell a massive portal like *www.excite.com, excite@home.com,* or *www.msn.com* about the thousands of people bidding for cuddly toys on your site.
14. Accept no less than $1 million from one of them to carry *huggablepuppies.com* on their Web site.

How to Make a Million, Part 2 ....

1. Have an interesting family that is always up for a laugh.
2. Purchase a cheap Web-TV camera and wire it into the top corner of your kitchen/living room.
3. Create an Internet homepage called *http://www.happysmithfamily.com.*
4. Plug your camera into the homepage, and go "live" on the Internet.

5. Tell everybody you know about your Web site. Make a fuss about it.

6. Arrange with everyone in your family to be fantastically nice to each other from 7 A.M. until 8:30 A.M. and from 3:30 P.M. until 8 P.M. Hug and kiss a lot. Call each other "Darling" and "Sweetheart." Laugh a lot.

7. Suddenly, unpredictably, after several days, at peak viewing time (about 6 P.M.), go ballistic. Have a HUGE FIGHT! Shout your guts out. Try to strangle each other. Then, gradually, get over it. Make friends again, weeping deeply. Return to normal smiling happiness.

8. Word will get around about this incredible family that is amazingly happy all the time, but just sometimes turn into monsters. This will keep viewers guessing. They will stay tuned for hours, hoping to see the action.

9. When you have thousands of "hits" an hour, hire an agency to sell advertisements.

10. Put the ad income into a bank account. Wait until it reaches $1 million.

How to Make a Million, Part 3 ....

1. Look around at what everybody is doing. Are they all living in houses? And are there more and more people all the time? If you answered "yes" to both questions, start a building firm by having business cards printed.

2. Acquire cheap land on the fringes of growing areas. Do something else for a few years until people are badgering you to sell your land for housing.

3. Get the land approved for building.

4. Get a bank to pay for putting up twelve hundred apartments.

5. Look around at what apartments are costing, and charge considerably more.

6. Retire.

How to Make a Million, Part 4 ....

1. Examine the sunshine records. Choose a place where it is getting sunnier because of global warming.

2. Contact factories by Internet, reserving 100,000 solar panels at a bargain price.
3. Write to ten million homes, offering an "unbeatable" deal on solar power. The deal is actually quite normal, and assures you a good profit on each unit.
4. Promise to deliver in six weeks.
5. One percent of homes will purchase (this is a scientific fact!). That means all your 100,000 units will sell. When they do, contact the factory and confirm the order.
6. Deliver the units.
7. Collect a million.

What to Do with Your $1 Million ....

Be an Angel

Place your money in a trust fund dedicated to people in crisis. Use the interest earned by the money to buy large batches of used clothes, blankets, eyeglasses, and medicine. Store them. Watch the TV news. Wait for a disaster, such as a typhoon, flood, famine, or earthquake. As soon as tragedy hits, hire a helicopter and send your supplies down to the area. Make sure an official working for an aid agency receives the goods. Give presentations to groups of good people about what you are doing. Encourage them to help.

Be a Devil

Get all your money together in a suitcase. Gloat over it. Leave the suitcase open on the floor and invite your friends in. Enjoy their jealousy. If one of them asks for a loan, tell them how sorry you are. Slam the suitcase shut on their fingers. Buy a gaudy-colored limo, hire a uniformed chauffeur, and drive around poor areas,

waving money out of the window at envious local people. Place a wallet crammed with $100 bills on the pavement outside your gate. Attach a piece of clear fishing line to it, and hide behind your hedge. When a passerby spies the money and bends down to pick it up, quickly pull the wallet back into your garden with a cackle of glee.

Be a Dreamer

Make your dreams come true. You have probably imagined being enormously successful. Hire a hall and five hundred out-of-work actors. Tell them what to do. Do a performance. When they give you a five-minute standing ovation, bow (or curtsy), blow kisses, blush, weep, point incredulously at yourself. Arrange for your favorite person to win the lottery by wiring up their radio and having an out-of-work actor announce their ticket number on the air. Have another out-of-work actor appear at their front door in a blazer marked "Lottery Officer," and hand over a huge wad of cash. Drop in at that moment, feign surprise, and enjoy their good fortune.

Be a Nuisance

Use your money to pester the kind of people you don't like. When your least favorite DJ comes on the radio, hire people to make hundreds of calls and jam up the radio-station switchboard. When your least favorite comedian is booked to appear at your local theater, buy all the tickets for one night. Sit alone in the front row, not laughing.

Buy an old wrecked car and park it permanently outside the house of the neighbor you don't like. Place advertisements in the newspapers giving the names of all the so-called celebrities you don't like. Nothing else, just their names and the fact that you don't like them. They can't sue you for that.

Be a Multimillionaire

Use your million to make millions more. Hire experts to advise you where to invest half your money at high risk, and half more safely. That's called "hedging your bets." If they double half your money, use it to do the same thing again. Use your million to borrow another million. Split both millions and invest them, hedging your bets. When you have five million, use it to raise another five million. Continue splitting and hedging your bets. Stop either when you have $500 million or when you are bored.

The Best Things in Life Are Free ....

So who needs a million anyway? If you're rich,
how can you tell real friends from people
who want your money? How do you deal
with the headache of making choices
all the time? How do you protect
your possessions? Some of the
best things in life are free.